ALICE WALKER

POWER OF THE PEN

BLACK WOMEN WRITERS

by Joyce Markovics

NORWOOD HOUSE PRESS

For more information about Norwood House Press, please visit our website at:
www.norwoodhousepress.com or call 866-565-2900.

Book Designer: Ed Morgan
Editorial and Production: Bowerbird Books

Library of Congress Cataloging-in-Publication Data

Names: Markovics, Joyce L., author.
Title: Alice Walker / by Joyce Markovics.
Description: [Buffalo] : Norwood House Press, 2024. | Series: Power of the
    pen : Black women writers | Includes bibliographical references and
    index. | Audience: Grades 4-6
Identifiers: LCCN 2023045955 (print) | LCCN 2023045956 (ebook) | ISBN
    9781684506736 (hardcover) | ISBN 9781684049721 (paperback) | ISBN
    9781684049783 (ebook)
Subjects: LCSH: Walker, Alice, 1944---Juvenile literature. | Authors,
    American--20th century--Biography--Juvenile literature. | Civil rights
    workers--United States--Biography--Juvenile literature. | Social
    reformers--United States--Biography--Juvenile literature. | African
    American authors--Biography--Juvenile literature. | LCGFT: Biographies.
    | Picture books.
Classification: LCC PS3573.A425 Z83 2024 (print) | LCC PS3573.A425
    (ebook) | DDC 813/.54 [B]--dc23
LC record available at https://lccn.loc.gov/2023045955
LC ebook record available at https://lccn.loc.gov/2023045956

372N--012024

Manufactured in the United States of America in North Mankato, Minnesota.

CONTENTS

INTRODUCING ALICE

> *The most healthy thing is to be true to your own self.*

Alice Walker is a powerful force. She writes heartfelt stories about the lives of Black people. One of her most famous books, *The Color Purple*, follows a Black woman who struggles to find her voice. The book won Alice the Pulitzer Prize for fiction. She became the first Black woman in history to win this award! Alice pushes her readers to open their minds and speak their truth. "You have a right to express what you see and what you feel and what you think," said Alice. "Be bold!"

ASK YOURSELF
WHY IS IT IMPORTANT FOR PEOPLE TO TELL THEIR STORIES?

Alice Walker isn't afraid to voice her opinions— even when people disagree with her.

BEST KNOWN FOR HER NOVELS, ALICE ALSO WRITES POEMS, ESSAYS, AND SHORT STORIES.

EARLY YEARS

> "My mother says I was writing before I was crawling. I wrote in the dirt with a twig."

Alice Malsenior Walker was born on February 9, 1944, near Eatonton, Georgia. She was the youngest of eight children. Her parents were **sharecroppers** on a **plantation**. The family lived in a small house with no electricity or indoor plumbing. Still, Alice's mother Minnie made the home beautiful. She hung colorful wallpaper in her children's room. "It was just part of my mother's magic," said Alice.

Sharecroppers in Eatonton, Georgia, a small farming town

The white plantation owner wanted Alice and her siblings to work in the fields. Minnie refused. Alice remembers her mom saying, "These children are my children, and they are going to be educated." "I will never forget that," said Alice.

Alice at age six

MANY OF THE BLACK PEOPLE WHO LIVED IN EATONTON WHEN ALICE WAS YOUNG WORKED AS SHARECROPPERS. MANY OF THEIR **ANCESTORS** HAD ESCAPED SLAVERY IN THE SOUTH. TODAY, SHARECROPPING IS VIEWED AS A FORM OF SLAVERY. THE WORK WAS HARD, AND THE PAYMENT WAS BARELY ENOUGH TO LIVE ON.

When Alice was only four years old, her mom put her in school. Little Alice loved learning. Then her young life changed in an instant. At age eight, Alice was playing outside with her brothers. By mistake, one brother shot her with a **BB gun**. A pellet landed in her right eye. "It was a blinding, massive sting," said Alice. By the time she saw a doctor, it was too late. Alice was blind in that eye.

Alice never got the sight back in her right eye. But that didn't stop her from writing.

Over time, Alice's accident led to something positive. While she healed, Alice read. She **devoured** every book she could. And she wrote too. "In each of us, there is a little voice that knows exactly which way to go," Alice said. "And I learned very early to listen to it."

ASK YOURSELF
CAN YOU REMEMBER THE FIRST STORY YOU WROTE? WHAT WAS IT ABOUT?

Alice's mom saved up to buy her daughter a typewriter. Alice never forgot this special gift.

> **For me, writing has always come out of living a fairly to-the-bone life, just really being present to a lot of life.**

Alice hungrily read and wrote. She became a star student. The schools in Eatonton were **segregated**. So, Alice went to the only high school Black students could attend. In 1961, Alice graduated as **valedictorian**. She earned a **scholarship** to Spelman College. Alice left for college with a suitcase, a sewing machine, and the typewriter from her mom. Her family beamed with pride.

Alice attended Butler-Baker High School in Eatonton.

In college, Alice was shy. "I said hardly a word in class," she later wrote. But she connected with her teacher Howard Zinn. Alice said, "He loved what he was teaching and clearly wanted his students to love it also. We did." Howard pushed his students to fight for their beliefs. Alice started finding her voice. She believed in equal rights for Black people and women. She was becoming an **activist**.

These are some of Spelman College's earliest graduates.

SPELMAN IS A HISTORICALLY BLACK COLLEGE FOR WOMEN IN ATLANTA, GEORGIA. IT WAS FOUNDED IN 1881.

HER WORK

After two years, Spelman no longer felt like a good fit for Alice. So, she switched to Sarah Lawrence College in New York. While there, she wrote poetry about the dark times in her life. Alice shared her poems with one of her teachers, Muriel Rukeyser. Muriel was wowed by the depth and feeling in Alice's poetry.

Alice got a full scholarship to attend Sarah Lawrence College. During the summers, she registered Black people to vote.

In 1965, Alice graduated from college. The same year, she met Melvyn Leventhal. He was a Jewish **civil rights** lawyer. They married in 1967. Soon after, the couple moved to Mississippi. There, Alice worked for the NAACP (National Association for the Advancement of Colored People). She taught history to Black women. And she wrote. In 1968, with Muriel's help, Alice **published** a book of her poems.

In 1969, Alice and Melvyn had a daughter named Rebecca. Rebecca became a writer like her mom.

ALICE AND MELVYN WERE THE FIRST LEGALLY MARRIED **INTERRACIAL** COUPLE IN MISSISSIPPI. THEY FACED THREATS FROM RACIST WHITE PEOPLE, INCLUDING THE **KKK**. ALICE CALLED **RACISM** A CREEPING VINE. SHE WROTE, "IF YOU DON'T KEEP PULLING UP THE ROOTS, IT WILL GROW BACK FASTER THAN YOU CAN DESTROY IT."

In 1970, Alice's first novel came out. It was called *The Third Life of Grange Copeland.* The book is about a sharecropper who abuses his family. It stemmed from a real story. "It was an incredibly difficult novel to write," said Alice. "I had to look at, and name, and speak up about violence among Black people."

Alice signs a copy of one of her books.

ASK YOURSELF
THINK ABOUT A DIFFICULT EXPERIENCE IN YOUR PAST. DO YOU THINK WRITING ABOUT IT WOULD MAKE YOU FEEL BETTER?

Then Alice moved to New York for a teaching job. All the while, she kept writing. In 1976, Alice and Melvyn **divorced**. That same year, Alice finished her next novel *Meridian*. It was the story of a young Black civil rights activist. Her name was Meridian Hill. In the book, Alice discusses her views on the civil rights movement. She also explores interracial love and being a Black American woman. Readers responded to the book's honesty.

In the 1963 March on Washington, Alice marched for civil rights with thousands of others.

In 1977, Alice moved to California. She settled in the small town of Boonville. That's where she began writing *The Color Purple*. The novel was based on her grandparents. "I wanted to spend time with them," Alice said. She wanted to bring their lost voices back into the world.

In 2004, *The Color Purple* was made into a play. Alice attended the opening.

The book follows the life of Celie, a young Black woman in the South. Celie faces a lot of abuse and **trauma**. But she rises above her struggles. And Celie **empowers** herself. The book was unlike anything that had ever been written. Alice's story deeply moved people. In 1983, the book won the National Book Award. It also won the Pulitzer Prize for fiction. Alice's life changed forever.

In 2015, *The Color Purple* returned to Broadway. It starred Jennifer Hudson (right) and Cynthia Erivo (middle).

THE COLOR PURPLE HAD CRITICS TOO. SOME PEOPLE THOUGHT IT WAS TOO VIOLENT. OTHERS THOUGHT IT PORTRAYED BLACK MEN IN A NEGATIVE WAY.

Not long after *The Color Purple* came out, it was made into a movie. Alice agreed to this because of her mother. Minnie was in poor health and unable to read the novel. And Alice wanted to share her story with her mom. In 1986, Alice's sister planned a screening of the movie in Eatonton. When Alice arrived, cheering crowds met her. Minnie was there too. She loved every minute of the film. Alice was overjoyed.

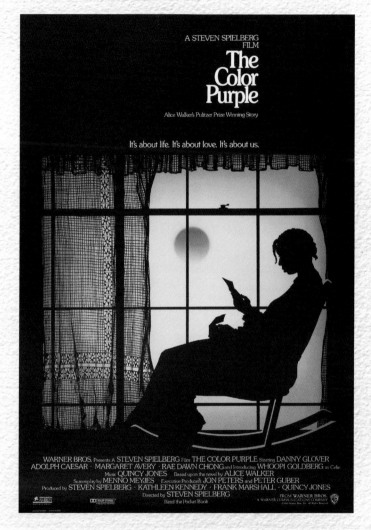

The Color Purple was a popular movie directed by Steven Spielberg.

> **You don't always have to be doing something. You can just be, and that's plenty.**

Zora Neale Hurston was a writer who spent her life studying and celebrating Black stories and culture.

After the success of *The Color Purple*, Alice kept writing. "The stories chase you," she once said. She wrote *In Search of Our Mothers' Gardens* next. It was a collection of 36 short pieces about Black women, including the writer Zora Neale Hurston. Alice continued writing. She wrote novels, poetry, and nonfiction. "I feel that I need to write what comes to me," said Alice.

IN RECENT YEARS, ALICE HAS VOICED **ANTI-SEMITIC** IDEAS. HATEFUL IDEAS HURT PEOPLE. BECAUSE OF WHAT ALICE HAS SAID, SOME PEOPLE HAVE STOPPED READING HER WORK.

ALICE'S POWER

> "The most common way people give up their power is by thinking they don't have any."

For almost her entire life, Alice Walker has been writing. She has written more than 40 books about the power of Black women. And she has no plans of stopping. Alice urges her readers to think differently. She believes every person should think, speak, and live freely—as she does. "What do Black women writers want?" she asks. "We want freedom," said Alice. "I will live the way that I want to the total extent that is possible." When Alice reflects on her life, she says, "I have no regrets." Her powerful words ring out.

ASK YOURSELF
WHAT DO YOU WANT TO
BE KNOWN FOR WHEN
YOU GROW UP?

Alice Walker is being honored at
a parade in San Francisco.

TIMELINE AND ACTIVITY

February 9, 1944
Alice is born near Eatonton, Georgia

1961
Alice graduates from high school as valedictorian

1965
Alice graduates from Sarah Lawrence College

1968
Alice publishes her first book, a collection of poetry

1982
Alice publishes *The Color Purple*

1983
Alice wins the Pulitzer Prize for fiction and the National Book Award

1983–Present
Alice publishes dozens of novels, poems, and short stories

GET WRITING!

Alice Walker is best known for her novels. But she also enjoys writing essays. Think about a topic that you feel strongly about. Then write a ten-sentence essay. Share your work with an adult or friend!

GLOSSARY

activist (AK-tuh-vist): a person who fights for a cause.

ancestors (AN-sess-turz): family members who lived a long time ago.

anti-Semitic (an-TEE-suh-MIT-ik): hostile or hateful toward Jewish people.

BB gun (BEE-bee GUHN): an air rifle that fires small pellets called BBs.

civil rights (SIV-uhl RITES): the rights everyone should have to freedom and equal treatment under the law, regardless of who they are.

devoured (dee-VOURD): read eagerly and quickly.

divorced (dih-VAWRSD): no longer married.

empowers (em-POU-erz): gives power or authority.

interracial (in-ter-REY-shuhl): involving people of different racial groups.

KKK (KAY-KAY-KAY): stands for the Ku Klux Klan; a group that uses fear and violence to hurt Black, Jewish, and other people.

plantation (plan-TAY-shuhn): a large farm where crops such as cotton or tea are grown.

published (PUHB-lishd): printed or made available for people to read.

racism (REY-siz-uhm): a system of beliefs and policies based on the idea that one race is better than another.

scholarship (SKOL-ur-ship): an award that pays for a person to go to college.

segregated (SEG-rih-gate-id): kept Black people separated from white people.

sharecroppers (SHAIR-krop-erz): farmers who give a part of each crop as rent.

trauma (TRAW-muh): a terrible physical or emotional experience, or the effects of it.

valedictorian (val-ih-dik-TAWR-ee-uhn): a student who does better than anyone else in school.

FOR MORE INFORMATION

Books

O'Neill, Bill. *The Great Book of Black Heroes*. Sheridan, WY: LAK Publishing, 2021.
Explore the lives of 30 incredible Black people.

Walker, Alice. *Sweet People Are Everywhere*. Miami, FL: Tra Publishing, 2021.
Alice Walker teaches young readers about kindness.

Websites

Britannica Kids: Alice Walker

(https://kids.britannica.com/students/article/Alice-Walker/314051#:~:text=Alice%20Malsenior%20
Walker%20was%20born,write%20instead%20of%20doing%20chores)
Learn about Alice Walker's Life.

PBS Learning Media: A Black Writer in the South

(https://ny.pbslearningmedia.org/resource/wal14.ela.lit.south/a-black-writer-in-the-south/)
In this video, Alice Walker shares stories from her childhood.

INDEX

ABOUT THE AUTHOR

Joyce Markovics has written hundreds of children's books. She's passionate about celebrating the lives and accomplishments of women. Joyce thanks Bill Ferris for contributing to this book.